Publish to Profit

"If you do what you've always done, you'll get what you've always gotten."

–**Tony Robbins**

Publish to Profit

**A Proven 4-Step System For Attracting
New Higher Paying Customers**

Keith Dougherty

XMS

Florida

Publish to Profit

Copyright © 2016 Keith Dougherty

All rights reserved.

XMS Publishing

1391 NW St Lucie West Blvd, Suite 247

Port St Lucie, FL 34986

This publication is designed to provide accurate and authoritative information regarding the subject matter covered. It is sold with the understanding that the publisher is not engaged in rendering legal, accounting, medical or other professional services.

The information and opinions presented in this book are intended for educational purposes only. Any income claims or results discussed in this book are not typical, and they are for example only.

ISBN-10: 0692672370
ISBN-13: 978-0692672372

Published in the United States of America

"Limitations live only in our minds. But if we use our imaginations, our possibilities become limitless." –Jamie Paolinetti

Dedication

This book is dedicated to all my awesome clients who strive each and every day to build an excellent business. To my wife who always supports me and stand behind everything I do, I love you. To my awesome kids, you are the reason that I do what I do.

I also dedicate this book to all of my wonderful clients and fans that helped make me a #1 best-selling author when my book debuted ahead of *Thing and Grow Rich* by Napoleon Hill.

Amazon Best Sellers
Our most popular products based on sales. Updated hourly.

‹ Any Department   Best Sellers in Home Based Small Businesses
‹ Kindle Store
   ‹ Kindle eBooks   Top 100 Paid   Top 100 Free
    ‹ Business & Investing
     Small Business &
     Entrepreneurship
     Bookkeeping
     Capital Generation
     Entrepreneurship
     Franchises
     Home Based
     Legal Guides
     Mail Order
     New Business
     Enterprises

1.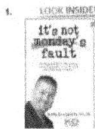
It's Not Monday's Fault
Discover How...
by Keith Dougherty
★★★★★ (12)
Kindle Edition
$0.99

2.
Make Money Online Volume
2 - 67 More
by Connie Brentford
★★★★★ (30)
Kindle Edition
$0.00 √Prime
$0.99

3.
The Classic Napoleon Hill
Masterpiece...
by Napoleon Hill
★★★★★ (55)
Kindle Edition
$0.99

BLOCK
THE ACID WITH

"Dream big and dare to fail."

–Norman Vaughan

What Others Say About
Working With Keith

"Keith my highest recommendation as someone you should definitely listen to."

I've worked with Keith on several successful promotions, and I've learned a lot from him. I can tell you first hand that he is a brilliant marketer who loves helping people and takes pride in providing real value to his students. But, the one thing that was refreshing about working with Keith was his integrity. He always delivered exactly what he promised with no surprises. That combination of experience and credibility gets Keith my highest recommendation as someone you should definitely listen to.

Ron Douglas, NY Times Best Selling Author
RonDouglas.com

"Keith's training was awesome."

Keith's training was awesome it gave me a whole new perspective on how we can utilize the internet beyond just marketing our website.

Kelli M. – Florida

"Thanks to Keith's training I received my first check."

I published my first "successful" book. After trying for almost a year and a half with very little success, I almost gave up. Now thanks to Keith's training I received my first check from my book.

Thank you, Keith Dougherty, for providing me with the tools and expertise necessary to finally make money from my books.

Cody Z. – Wisconsin

"Keith is an awesome teacher."

Keith is an awesome teacher. This was the most amazing training.

Beth W. – Hawaii

"The training is superb and so most helpful!"

I like the coaching style so, so much! Keith explains the stuff into the little details, and he is never tired of our questions! He shows his secrets and his knowledge, every piece. The training is superb and so most helpful! Thank you, Keith, I have the feeling I got the key to success!

Jac E. – Germany

"Keith is amazing and gives endlessly of himself and his expertise."

This is beyond a doubt the absolutely best training I have ever received! Keith is amazing and gives endlessly of himself and his expertise.

Margie S. – Maryland

"Keith's level of detail and support is excellent."

The training that Keith provides is both detailed and informative. Keith is dedicated to making sure his clients understand and can put the things that are taught into action. Keith's teaching style is awesome. I would attend any course Keith teaches. Keith's level of detail and support is excellent. Thanks so much.

David W. – Texas

Table of Contents

Introduction

"Whatever the mind of man can conceive and believe, it can achieve." – Napoleon Hill

Welcome to Publish to Profit.

February 7th, 2010, that day probably does not mean much to you, but to me, that was the very first time I published a book. It was a whole new world for me, and the experience was like nothing else. What made it even more real was when the actual book came in the mail. When I ripped open that cardboard box and saw my very first book. Seeing my name on it, turning the pages, realizing that after many years of wanting to publish a book, my dream had become a reality.

Since then I have gone on to publish over 100 books, and I have taught hundreds of people around the world to do the same. From 10-year-olds to people in their 90's. Everyone has a book inside of them, and there are many purposes for your book.

I wanted to take a moment here to make some promises to you for what you can expect from this book.

First Promise: Is to engage you to take action. You will have opportunities to gain access to expanded training and even talk with me to get your very own success blueprint to implementing your very own profit pulling book.

Second Promise: Is to show you as a business owner how you can use your very own book to engage your target market to help to elevate you as the go-to authority and expert in your niche. This will allow you to get more leads, get more customers, and command premium prices.

Third Promise: Is to encourage you to you to take action and implement. Everything is a process, and you will discover a proven process here. But, if you were looking for some quick and easy way to generate more leads, more business, and higher profits this is not it. You do have to take action and implement the system.

Fourth Promise: That you are not here to see the next USA Today or NY Times Bestseller. The intention of this book is to allow us a chance to get to know each other, develop rapport and see if at some point we are a good fit for future projects together.

Fifth Promise: Is to pack this book with as much useful content as possible. You will discover multiple ways to promote yourself with books, and leverage the latest technology available to set yourself for long-term growth.

The primary objective of this book is to give you the strategy behind using books in your business. This is more of the why than the exact how-to process. We do have other programs available that do have exact step-by-step instructions for implement everything you will learn in this book.

You might even be saying, why are you giving away this strategy, what is the catch. The simple answer is yes I do have a motive. To be honest, I want you to think, wow if Keith gives away this kind of insight and strategies for free, imagine what it would be like if I signed up for one of his course or worked with him.

If after going through this book and you enjoy the content, I certainly welcome your feedback. You can connect with me on Facebook here:

https://www.facebook.com/keithdoughertymarketing/

The best way for us to connect would be for you to use the link below and get access to more content and details on how to use this method to grow your business.

I look forward to connecting with you and helping you grow your business.

Keith Dougherty

FREE VIDEO TRAINING AND BOOK UPDATES
As things change so do we, to make sure you are always up-to-date on how you can grow your business with a book, make sure you visit the link below.

Visit: PublishToProfitBook.com/bonus

Main Benefits of Writing a Book

"Strive not to be a success, but rather to
be of value." –Albert Einstein

In this chapter, we are going to look at the benefits of becoming an author and what it means for you and your business. Now keep in mind this isn't about becoming the next JK Rowling's or any famous author you can think of. What we will be talking about primarily is how you can write your own book and boost your sales and increase your income.

One of the first ways writing a book helps you, and your business is that a book gives you more credibility. If you look around you, and you think of people that you consider experts why do you consider them an expert. Most of the time when someone sees that an individual has published a book on a certain topic that leads them to believe that that person is an expert on that topic. If you go to Amazon, and you type in a particular subject say how to hire salespeople. You're going to see a bunch of different books regarding this subject of how to hire salespeople. The perception in today's culture is to assume, and yes I know what the word assume can mean, but what you have to realize here is that people perceive you as the expert when you have the book. You are viewed as a credible source and an authority figure in that market.

I have personally used this exact method to increase my consulting business time and time again. I wrote a book in the area that I wanted to focus on; then I would Target potential clients in that Market Place. Whenever I submitted a proposal to a potential client, I gave them all the standard items that you would normally expect to see, a proposal, a business card, any other information to back up my presentation. But then I would finish the call with my book. I would take the book out I would autograph the book, and then they're left with my entire package and when they sit down to compare that package to all the other proposals that they have received who's do you think is going to stand out more.

To jump back a little I, want to talk about why I used the word autograph versus the word sign. As a business person, everybody signs things like proposals checks paperwork things of that nature. But who autographs things? The word autograph is reserved for people that are famous, so by using that verbiage that helps position me even more in the potential clients I that I'm not just a regular consultant but that I am an expert and authority figure and potentially even a celebrity in that market. Can you see how this can help you stand out from your competition when you're trying to gain new business?

Another way you can utilize your book is to use it to get your foot in the door with a potential client. There're a few different ways that you can implement this tactic but to me, the easiest is to utilize Amazon directly. Once your book is published and live on Amazon you can go in and order a copy of your book and have it sent anywhere you like as a gift. How many people do you think don't like to receive gifts in the mail especially surprise gifts that they aren't even expecting? So I'll order a copy of my book, and I'll have it sent directly to a CEO or decision maker of a company that I'm trying to get in the door with. The great thing with Amazon is that actually gift wrap your item. So when the potential client receives this item from Amazon they open it and inside the box is a wrapped present. Of course, we also include a nice little note saying that we thought they couldn't gain value from having our book, so we had one sent directly to them as a gift.

What do you think might happen when I follow up with that business the following week? I typically will call and request to speak with the person I sent the item to. The main reason I'm calling is just to confirm that they received the gift. Nine times out of ten that person will get on the phone with you and speak to you and thank you for sending them a gift. On a side note, how many books have you ever thrown away in your lifetime? I want you to think about that because books stand the test of time, people don't just take a book and throw it away. So even if you can't sign that client immediately, your book is going to stay with them potentially forever.

What other marketing tool can you use to achieve this kind of impact? When I speak to them on the phone, I usually have one question for them. My one question is what is the biggest problem you have in your business today that you'd like to solve? Once I ask that question, I close my mouth, and I let them just speak. Let them tell you everything that's on their mind and exactly what their problem is. Most of the time they're going to open up, and they're going to give you precisely what they're having the most issue with. If have done your homework on your target market, then you should already know what they are going to say. This allows you to prepare how you can help them. After they tell you their major issue or issues, then you can offer your free advice.

This goes back to one of the teachings that I've found from a very popular and successful direct copy marketer named Frank Kern and he calls it results in advance. If I can give them a tactic or a strategy that they can take away that can potentially help them with their situation they're going to think even more favorably of me on top of that I just gave them that free book. So I offer the solution and then I say to them would you like me to help you implement it. This is a very powerful sales tactic that's not considered to be a high pressured sales tactic. This is about giving extreme value and offering to help someone before they become your client.

So to recap a book can:

- Give You Credibility

- Give You Free Advertising

- Help Differentiate You from the Competition

- Open Doors to New Prospects or Clients

"The simple truth is if you aren't deliberately, systematically, methodically or rapidly and dramatically establishing yourself as a celebrity, at least to your clientele and target market, you're asleep at the wheel, ignoring what is fueling the entire economy around you, neglecting development of a measurable valuable asset."

–Dan Kennedy

Step 1 – Research and Planning

*"You miss 100% of the shots you
don't take."* –Wayne Gretzky

When you are building a house, you have to lay the proper foundation for it to come out the way you want. You normally get blueprints, and they used throughout the entire project. A book is no different you can't publish or promote anything until we lay the proper foundation.

During this research and planning phase, we need to think about some fundamental questions.

Why are you writing this book in the first place?

You have to know your why so that you can plan the book around that. Are you trying to get more business, maybe get speaking engagements, maybe you want just to build an email list? You need to get clear on your why.

One thing to think about here is to ask yourself, "Why do I do what I do?" Why did you start your business, how do you help others? If you begin to look at this at a deep level, it will expose your why, your passion, and this is what we want to build on.

Who are you trying to attract to your business?

Ideally, if you have been in business any amount of time, you should be able to identify your ideal prospect. What I always tell my students is that you want to think back and remember those customers that were your absolute best. The one's that were easy to work with, spent a lot of money with you, and gave you a glowing recommendation. The made the process fun and easy. Think about those people and then write down specifics about them. Is there a particular age range they fall in, certain other demographics that they can be categorized in? Try and find all the common denominators. If you can do this, you can position your book to speak to your ideal customers.

How to Identify Your Target Market

There are three areas that we want to look at when it comes to identifying your target market. You might think you know what this is, but sometimes when you take a closer look, you will discover that there are sub-markets within a market. The deeper you can dive into understanding the market the better your message is going to be. Also, the more specialized you are, the more money you can potentially make.

Some would think that the broader appeal you have to a bigger market the more money you could make right? Well, that is not entirely accurate. Let's take the example of your general practice or family doctor. They are a generalist, serving the entire population of anyone who wants to come to them. They do not specialize in any one part of healthcare. You usually will see them first and then they refer you to what, a specialist. So when you have an issue with your foot, they refer you to the podiatrist, who is a specialist and only deals with feet. So they focus on one small area of the body. And if you have ever gone to a specialist, you know their fees are a lot higher than your family doctor. The more you know and the more specific you can get about one particular area, the more you can charge for your specialty.

The quicker you can find you ideal sub-market and what people need; you can elevate yourself to that specialist level. On top of that, once you publish your book, you are going to be able to position yourself.

Digging Deep into Your Market

- What are their biggest pains?
- What are their biggest passions?
- What do they desire the most?
- What do they think about?
- What do they search for online?
- What magazines do they read?

The more you can answer about your market the better you can serve them. If you can get into someone's head and know all of these, you are going to be able to connect with them on a much deeper level. The more of a connection you make, the more they will get to know, like and trust you. That leads to them wanting to do business with you.

The next thing you want to think about is:

Where do they hang out?

Things to look for are:

- Where do they spend time?
- What email newsletters to they read?
- What blogs do they frequent?
- What Facebook™ groups are they in?
- What keywords do they type into Google?
- What books to they buy on Amazon?

The more of these questions you can answer, the better you will understand where to find them. Once we know them inside and out, and we know we have our message, we have to be able to get that message in front of them to attract them to you and your business.

Using this method takes time and might not be the quickest path to success, but if you want to build a real long term business and do it right, you will use this strategy.

The other things we are going to have to look at while planning out our book would include:

- Your title and subtitle
- Your book cover

- Setting a hard deadline (this helps me stay on track)

How To Title Your Book For Success

Let's look at your title and subtitle and how you can come up with something to catch the attention of your ideal customer. This won't be as hard as you might think. One of the best things we can do is model after books that have already done well. Why reinvent the wheel, right?

You can head over to Amazon.com and go to the book section and take a look at the bestselling books in the category you want to associate yourself with. Let's say you wanted to be in the business category. One of the #1 bestselling books of all time is *The 7 Habits of Highly Effective People*, by Stephen Covey, Ph.D.

Think, how could you use this for yourself? All you have to do is just break down the title and turn it into a template

The 7 Secrets of Highly Effective People becomes…

The _____ Secrets of Highly Effective _____

Now you just use that template for your business. Let's say you are in the financial planning business. You could use one of these:

The 5 Secrets of Highly Effective Financial Planners

or

The 3 Secrets that Highly Effective Financial Planners Use to Increase Your Retirement by 125%

or

The 7 Secrets of Highly Successful Financial Planners

It does not have to be this title; you can do this with any title you find on Amazon®. Keep in mind though some brands might have a trademark, so you will want to double check that. I am not an attorney, and I don't pretend to be one in this book.

Let's take a look at another example. *The Da Vinci Code* by Dan Brown has sold over 80 million copies. We break it down just like we did the other one.

You could use this:

The _____ Code

The Home Sellers Code (If you were a real estate agent)

or

The Retirement Code (If you were a financial planner)

As you can see, you can take just about any book title and convert it to something that would relate to your business. Find the book title you like and modify it to fit your market.

Step 2 – Create Your Book

"The most difficult thing is the decision to act, the rest is merely tenacity." –Amelia Earhart

Now it is time to create your book. I am going to give you two methods that you can use to generate content that your ideal customer wants to see. I am also going to give you a one of the best-kept secrets here, especially if you don't like typing. I am not a big fan of writing, and I use this method all the time. First, let's look at the methods you can use.

Method 1 – From A to Point Z

One of the ways I will help my clients with this process is to look at the way you run your business. Do you have a certain process for doing something? Just like the book you are reading here, I sat down and said to myself "How can I teach people how to write a book and build more business from it." I then mapped out the process, step 1, step 2 and so on. You can use that same type of system if that fits you and your business.

I like using a mind map tool to gather my thoughts and give me an outline to follow when I am putting a book together. I use a free tool you can download online called xMind. (http://www.xmind.net/) Here is a sample outline. (See figure 1)

Figure 1

Method 2 – Frequently Asked Questions (FAQ) / Should Ask Questions (SAQ)

Now if you don't want to use the step by step format, you can turn to another method that works just as good. I did not invent this method, but I have used it for years to create tons of compelling content for my clients and myself.

Here is how it works. You sit down either with a pad a paper and a pen or on the computer. Make a list of as many FAQ's (frequently asked questions) you can think that your potential customers might ask of you. These are typically going to be about what people might ask you when they want to learn more about your area of expertise, not about your product or services.

The goal here is to educate, not to sell. You want to talk about the prospect and not yourself. All content should be directed to help them. You do not want this to come off as a sales pitch; it will turn people off. When you do this right, you will engage people, and they will feel a connecting with you. Ideally, if you can get anywhere from 8-10 FAQ's that is great.

Next, sit down and write as many SAQ's (should ask questions) that you can think of that your customer should be asking someone in your profession. These are the questions that you wish people would ask because it is the stuff they should be looking at, but might not consider or be thinking about. These questions help you stand out from your competition, and it helps position you even better with new customers.

If you don't want to type your book out, you can simply take your outline or the FAQ's and SAQ's that we created, and you can record yourself as you speak the content. Cool huh? You can use your phone or a voice recorder on the computer, then just send out the audio file for transcription and you have all of your content created for you without typing anything.

Once the content comes back, you can organize and format it in a book template. A typical book is 6"x9".

You might be asking, "How long does this book have to be?" There is not a right or wrong answer. If you record the content for you book and it takes you about an hour you will get anywhere from a 40-50 page book. Keep in mind you are not writing a novel here, the book's sole purpose is to establish your credibility and authority in your marketplace. You want to give highly relevant information and keep it as short as possible. People want to get the information quickly and easily. That faster you can deliver the message, the better off you will be.

One major point I would like to make here is that you want to become an educator and an advocate for your prospects. When someone feels that you understand them and what they are going through, they are going to be more likely to want to work with you.

Remember in the previous chapter we talked about really understanding your target market. To know their ins and outs, to understand their pain, to know where they hang out. That is why that is so important in this process.

You don't want to be all things to everybody; you want to be the go-to person for your specialty. Remember earlier we talked about the doctor analogy. The difference between a general practice doctor and a specialist. You want to become the expert.

CREATING TIPS AND INSPIRATION

Maybe you already know the purpose of your book, or even written part of it. We can help you at any point you are at. We actually have a proven process to help get you up and running quickly and easily.

Visit: PublishToProfitBook.com/bonus

Step 3 – Publish Your Book

"Your time is limited, so don't waste it living someone else's life." –Steve Jobs

Now that you have everything ready to go, your cover and your content you are ready to publish your book and let the world know about you.

I want you to keep in mind that ideally, you can publish your book in the traditional format, but there are many other ways you can benefit from the content you have created in this book.

The very first place you can publish your book is on Amazon. They have both the Kindle (digital) side of the house and with Createspace (physical) side. The great thing, you are not charged anything to publish your book on both of these platforms. They even will pay you up to 70% royalties when your books sell and if you book does well, they will help promote it for you.

Another benefit of using Amazon is that they give you your very own "Author Page" that allows you to add pictures, videos, schedule events, have a full bio and links to all of your books. They love endorsing their authors. The most successful you are, the more they are too, it only makes sense.

If you are looking for further distribution, you can also publish your book on Apple iBooks, Barnes and Noble, Kobo, Tolino, Odilo, Inkter, Askews & Holts, Browns Books, Bake & Tayler and many others. For these, you need to use a publishing company such as Bookbaby.

The actual step-by-step details on how to format your book is a little beyond the scope of this book. But, I will cover some basics for you if you want to tackle this on your own. For Kindle and Createspace you can use Microsoft Word. Once you have the file, you upload it to Kindle and

Createspace. I would double check the screen view to make sure you don't need to adjust any pages.

Both Kindle and Createspace have publishing guidelines that you have to follow. Make sure you read those and stay within the rules so that you book does not get held up on technical issues.

Ideally, this is what we do best. I always use the analogy; you would not try and pull your tooth at home or perform Lasik eye surgery on yourself. Well, at least, I hope wouldn't unless you are a professional. We make it our point to know how to format, how to construct and how to publish books for maximum success.

We do have one of the best "Done With You" service on the market. And of course, when you work with us, you are guaranteed to get your book written, published and become a bestseller in under 30 days.

Ok enough with my shameless plug about our services, I am just really passionate about helping businesses use these methods and achieve the best possible results.

PUBLISHING TIPS AND INSPIRATION

Maybe you already know the purpose of your book, or even written part of it. We can help you at any point you are at. We actually have a proven process to help get you up and running quickly and easily.

Visit: PublishToProfitBook.com/bonus

Step 4 – Profit From Your Book

"I am not a product of my circumstances. I am a product of my decisions." –Stephen Covey

Now you are a published author; the royalty checks should start pouring in right? Unfortunately, it does not quite work that way unless you are JK Rowling or James Paterson. As a matter of fact, Forbes Magazine recently put out an article that between 600,000 to 1,000,000 books are published every year in the U.S. alone, but most sell fewer than 250 copies in their lifetime, depending on the distribution method.

Are you serious!?

The plain and simple truth is that the money you make in publishing does not come from royalty checks. I did not design this business model to sell books for the sake of selling them; I designed it to allow you to grow your business in a consistent and substantial manner without the hassle of having to hard sell anyone.

The real power of this system comes in the systems or as some would call it the sales funnels that run behind the scenes. Your book is just a frontend tool; a means to attract people into your system and let the backend system do its job to get you highly qualified prospects that want to do business with you.

The bottom line is yes; you can make money with royalties would you rather make $0.99 - $2.99 or would you rather make $100, $1,000 or more every time you sell or give one of your books away.

Let's take a look at other ways and different strategies that we use ourselves and that we teach our clients to use so that they can earn more with their books.

Book Profit #1: Building Email Lists and Sales

The first way you can use your book to make a profit is to set up systems where you can collect emails as well as generate sales directly from that system.

Mostly this process, in the marketing world, is called a sales funnel. The easiest way to facilitate building an email list from when your book is sold it to entice the reader to come to a page that you control. Normally the best way to do that is to offer something of significant value, that is related to your book content, that the user can get more value from you and want access to it.

Some ideas of things you could offer would be:

- Checklist
- Cheat Sheet
- Blueprint
- Resource List
- Video Training
- Software / Free Trial
- Discount / Free Shipping
- Quiz / Survey
- Assessment / Test

As you can see, there are lots of ideas on what to offer. Let's say that you are a financial planner. You could provide a checklist of things you should be doing for your retirement planning. You could also provide a quick quiz and say, "Are you ready for retirement?", take this quick 2-minute quiz to find out.

The great thing with all of these possible ideas is that you are offering, even more, value for your reader. You are giving more and helping people along a path. The path could lead to them becoming a client or customer of yours, but you are guiding them in a very caring fashion.

One of the reasons I like to use video, whether it is an in-person video or just a simple screen capture video, is that people get to hear your voice and connect with your personality even more. The more people know, like, and trust you, the more inclined they will be to want to do business with you.

Here is the simple system broken down so you can see it visually.

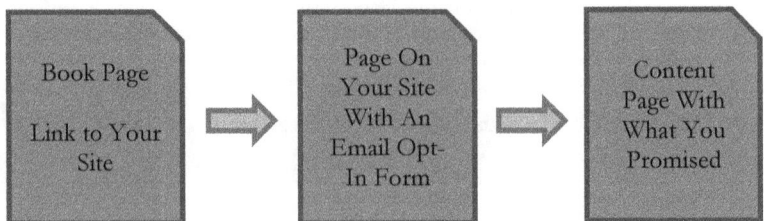

Book Page Link to Your Site	⇒	Page On Your Site With An Email Opt-In Form	⇒	Content Page With What You Promised

Book Profit #2: An In-Demand Consultant

Being an in-demand consultant is one of the easiest ways you can use the book. Think back to when we talked about the benefits of being a published author. Here is a quick recap for you:

1. Instant Credibility
2. Instant Authority (Think what adding bestselling author does to this.)
3. Stand-Out from Your Competition
4. Opening Doors to Decision Makers
5. Published Authors make more money and help more people

With an expert authority book, let's first look at what is consider an expert. The simple definition from Wikipedia states:

An expert is someone widely recognized as a reliable source of technique or skill whose faculty for judging or deciding rightly, justly, or wisely is accorded authority and status by their peers or the public in a specific well-distinguished domain.

An expert, more generally, is a person with extensive knowledge or ability based on research, experience, or occupation and in a particular area of study.

An expert can be, by virtue of credential, training, education, profession, publication or experience, believed to have special knowledge of a subject beyond that of the average person, sufficient that others may officially (and legally) rely upon the individual's opinion.

If you are a consultant in any field, and you have a book on the subject, that is instantly going to make you stand out from all the noise in the market. Everyone is doing the same thing when it comes to marketing. The book not only helps you stand out, but it also helps you stand up and become the obvious choice. People want to work with the best.

Book Profit #3: Freelance Writer

This method might seem a little weird to you at first, but it works extremely well. Let's walk through an example and I think it will make sense quickly.

Let's say you're a consultant, and you like working with lawyers. Now calling them up might be difficult and trying to get them on the phone and attempt to pitch your service to them, no matter how good you are. What if you call and say, "Hello gatekeeper, this is Keith Dougherty, and I am writing a book on selecting the ideal personal injury attorney, and I would like to interview Mr. Top Lawyer on the subject, could I please speak to him. What do you think will happen nine times out of ten? They will get on the phone with you, right?

Ok, so now you have them on the phone, now what. You explain that you are putting together a book on selecting the ideal personal injury attorney, and based on their stellar reputation you want to get their input as an industry expert. No matter who you are talking to, you are stroking their ego here; everyone wants to be thought of as the industry expert. Ask them the question you have. Mr. Top Lawyer, what are the top 3 things that a person should look at when they need a personal injury lawyer. Then just let them talk. I will usually record the interview, so I don't miss out on what they are saying. Then confirm their information, as in their name, website, and phone. Tell them that way anyone who reads the book will be able to contact them. Then you simply thank them for their time and let them know when the book is out, you will let them know.

Now, you might be saying, wait how the heck does that get me more business as a consultant. You have to remember this is a process. It is one of building rapport, delivering value and showing them you are great to work with and deliver on what you promise.

I would do this with the top ten personal injury lawyers that you would like to potentially have as clients. Take all of the information and put it together in a quick book. Publish it to Kindle. Now you have done exactly what you said you were going to do, right? Now comes the fun part.

You call each of the lawyers back up, and of course, they take your call because you are not the consultant, but you are the freelance writer publishing a book including them in it. I let them know that the book is live, and I will be sending over a link for them to view it on Amazon. Now I have done something for them as I promised. I then usually say, can I ask you a quick question? They always say sure. Then I ask them this, "What is your biggest problem with your business right now? You will be amazed and how quickly, at least, the right business owners, will come back with a response. Just listen and take it all in. If you know your market, which as a good consultant you should, you should be able to know what they are going to say. It should be either, well we are always trying to bring in new business, or we are overwhelmed with clients and we are attempting to grow. But, it should be something that you should know.

There are not that many different problems that business owners face. Usually either they are trying to get more business, or if they are smart, they are attempting to increase their profit margins.

Now you can step in and say, Mr. Top Lawyer, it just so happens that not only am I a freelance writer, I help law firms... You get the idea you offer how you can help them here. It's now time to step in and be that consultant.

Book Profit #4: Speaking From Stage

One of the great benefits of having a published book is it will allow you to get paid speaking gigs. Let's think about this, if somebody's going to have a meeting and they want to hire a speaker who do you think they would rather have to speak? Someone that might know about the topic or a published author, or even better yet a number one best-selling author. You would have had to run a promotion for your book and got it to number one status, and that's what happens when all my clients work with us. But even if you didn't have that, having a published book as we talked about before elevates you to that authority figure status.

When you speak, you're going to most likely be speaking to a high-value audience some of the people may have paid to be in the room where you're speaking. Now ideally, you would want to engage speaking gigs that are within your market. It doesn't make sense to speak to lawyers if you're ideal client is a real estate agent. You want to align yourself within your marketplace and a great place to do this is through associations. I'm talking about national and local organizations that most industries have. You can reach out to them and offer them your book as well as offer to speak, and you can decide if you'd like to charge a fee. Me personally if I can get in a room full of prospects that can potentially generate more business for my company I'll personally waive the speaking fee.

Now an interesting tactic you could use is some companies will say that they don't have a budget for an event for you to speak. Most companies do have training budgets. So what you can do as an alternate method is ask them how many people will be at the event and then offer for them to purchase those amount of copies of your book at whatever price you set it at. So let's say your book is normally $29.99, and there're a hundred people there so then you would be charging just under $3,000 to give your speech. Now the great thing there is the company can write it off as a training expense, and you get paid to speak as well as you're presenting to other people that are your potential prospects to grow your business.

Book Profit #5: Local Community and Events

This is another great method especially for building more Authority more celebrity and more notoriety in the local Marketplace. Once you write your book, you want to read your book about a specific process that's going to help your ideal prospect that you want to attract. You could then take that process and turn it into an actual course that you would teach people. You could teach this course via online electronic webinars, trove Workshop, or through PDF and mixed training.

Then what you could do is schedule local events. There are many different sites that offer local event scheduling, in fact one of the most popular ones is meetup.com. You can give away a copy of your book to anybody that signs up to come to the local event. Then when people are at the actual event you can help them with their process you can give them as we talked about it earlier results in advance and then you could offer them your course if they want more in-depth training.

You could also create an automated system online that offers your book for free and then you could bring people into a webinar which gives them some great training that would help move them in the right direction and then offer them your course as well at the end of that training session.

The power of this method is that you are not only a published author, actually, I'm a number one best selling author, but you're also now speaking in front of a group which elevates your success and your level of a celebrity even more. When people see you on a stage giving a presentation, you are the speaker you are the one in control of the room. This automatically increases your expert status even more.

Book Profit #6: Target Influencers

Targeting influencers might seem a little odd at first, but let me walk you through exactly how you can use this profit method. Here's a perfect example of how you could use an influencer to impact an audience of what you're trying to do. Let's say that you want to attract real estate agents into your Consulting business. You could reach out to real estate brokers that run the entire agency. What that means is they have real estate agents that work for them. Interview them and put them in your book. Let's say you're reading a book about real estate how to get more listings how to build a real estate career anything like that that's related to that market, and then you're going to interview the broker and ask them questions.

You might be saying to yourself guitar exactly am I going to generate revenue from trying to Target real estate agents and I'm interviewing brokers. Is it a broker is an influencer they have influence over their entire brokerage and potentially a lot of real estate agents. Ideally, when the book comes out, most people are going to want to tell others that they're part of a book. It goes into the ego, they want to feel valued and important, and they can say that I was featured in this book. So when their agents look at the book and the book is specifically designed to attract real estate agent you're going to have instant traffic to you to your system.

The big takeaway here is they gained prominence by being featured in your book plus they can provide their audience a new and useful information through your book. There is a good chance too that they may even buy copies for their entire brokerage and give them to every real estate agent that's there.

Book Profit #7: Engage the Local Media

Engaging the local media is another great way to get more exposure and elevate your status. The idea is that you want to become the local news story. What this would entail is either writing a press release yourself or having one written up for you. As a side note this is a service that we offer our clients. The press release is going to cover how you released a new book and it is available for sale on Amazon. This in itself will get you good coverage, but it works even better if you can say that not only published a new book, but become a best selling author as well.

You'll submit a news release out to a news propagation source that will be sent out to many different local affiliates of NBC, CBS, FOX, basically all the standard major network affiliate sites. What you can then do is take some of those links or the actual press release and get a hold of your local newspaper as well as the local TV stations and offer to do an interview and potentially get more publicity from the new book.

Obviously, this will lead to more people being aware of what you do that you are an expert in your field. Not only by having the book but with not being interviewed on TV, this will elevate public perception even more. When you establish this kind of credibility people want to with you. They want to work with the industry expert.

Another way to take advantage of this even further is setup an easy to remember domain name. Something like the one I have publishtoprofitbook.com. So when I do interviews, I can say, to get a copy of my book go here.

Ideally, at that page, you should be collecting emails and making it so people can get a copy of your book quickly and easily. Remember the more people that get your book, the better chance you have a getting more business.

How To Become a Best Selling Author

"The only person you are destined to become is the person
you decide to be." –Ralph Waldo Emerson

Ok, we have taken the journey to get here, you have identified you big why, you have pulled out your ideal prospect, gotten your content together and published your book. Now it is time to launch yourself into hopefully bestseller status.

Now just to clarify, Amazon determines a bestseller as any book that ranks in the top 100 of any of its categories.

And there are tons of categories. You ideally want to pick the ones that are most related to your market.

Over the years, we have been able to reverse-engineer Amazon's algorithm, and we can usually predict with pretty close accuracy how many books you need to sell in a one-day timeframe to become a #1 bestseller in your category. From general terms, it can be anywhere from 40-200 in a single day to hit #1 bestseller status.

Just to put this in perspective compared to say becoming a NY Times #1 bestseller. It would take an estimated 7,500-12,000 sales during a week to achieve that feat. You had better hope the week you pick that some huge celebrity did not decide to launch their book. Otherwise, you will be out of luck for sure.

One thing to keep in mind. The major premise and goal behind this book is not necessary to sell books. The goal is to get your book content out there and get in the hands of people that are potential prospects for your business.

Now if you want to make this book a marketing tool, you want to make sure that every chapter in the book has a call to action. Just like you have seen in this book, I give you an opportunity to connect with me numerous times. I offer free videos and more detailed training for you to come to my site.

Ideally, you will want to have a website setup that you can direct all of the people that read your book into your sales system (or some will call it a sales funnel). Using this method is a way which will help you automate your prospects process and get the right people in front of you.

BECOMING A BEST SELLER QUICKLY

If you don't want to struggle through trying to become a best selling author, let us help you out. We actually have a proven process to help get you best seller status quickly and easily.

Visit: <u>PublishToProfitBook.com/bonus</u>

It was a proud moment for me when this book was released, and we beat out marketing expert and serial entrepreneur Gary Vaynerchuk. On top fo that we also beat out Shark Tank's Daymond John. It was an excellent day, and I am very thankful to all that supported this book during its initial launch.

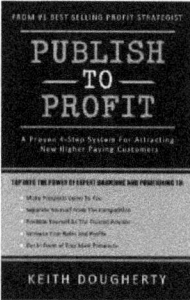

Not only did we beat them out, but we also were #1 in 3 different categories. (*We can do this for you too if you want, just reach out and get in contact with me.*)

Amazon Best Sellers

Our most popular products based on sales. Updated hourly.

Any Department
Kindle Store
Kindle eBooks
Business & Money
Entrepreneurship & Small Business
Bookkeeping
Entrepreneurship
Home-Based
Mail Order
Marketing
Small Business
Starting a Business

Best Sellers in Marketing for Small Businesses

Top 100 Paid   Top 100 Free

1.

Publish to Profit: A Proven 4-Step Sy...
by Keith Dougherty
★★★★☆ (3)
Kindle Edition
$0.99

2.

#AskGaryVee: One Entrepreneur's Take
by Gary Vaynerchuk
★★★★★ (212)
Kindle Edition
$16.99

3.

The Power of Broke: How Empty Pockets...
by Daymond John
★★★★☆ (155)
Kindle Edition
$13.99

4.

Jab, Jab, Jab, Right Hook: How to Tel...
by Gary Vaynerchuk
★★★★☆ (877)
Kindle Edition
$16.99

5.

Launch: An Internet Millionaire's Sec...
by Jeff Walker
★★★★☆ (968)
Kindle Edition
$8.99

6. kindleunlimited

Linked to Influence: 7 Powerful Rules...
by Stephanie Sammons
★★★★★ (39)
Kindle Edition
$5.99

Publish to Profit: A Proven 4-Step System For Attracting New Higher Paying Customers
Mar 19, 2016 | Kindle eBook
by Keith Dougherty

$0.99 Kindle Edition

Buy now with 1-Click ®

Auto-delivered wirelessly

★★★★☆ ▾ 3

#1 Best Seller in Marketing for Small Businesses

Sold by: Amazon Digital Services LLC

60

Conclusion

"Go confidently in the direction of your dreams. Live the life you have imagined." –Henry David Thoreau

If you got to this point you've been through the entire book and I think you can really see the major benefits of water book and do for you and your business. To recap for you one of the major things a book will do for you obviously is leverage and create credibility. From perception standpoint people that write books and once they become published books, the general public will typically perceive that person as an expert or authority figure in their Market. And the huge value of increasing your credibility is that more people will trust you. The more people that trust you the more people that are likely to do business with you which in turn this can increase your sales.

What are the other major ways that we talked about which I think is extremely important is differentiating your cell from your competition. But having a book most of your competitors are not going to be a published author. So from a prospect point of view when they're comparing two different or two or three different people for a given project by leaving your autographed copy of your book Within that is really going to help you stand out from your competition and potentially get more business.

Also one of the other ways that we talked about was that a book can open doors for you. It's a way that you can get access to potential clients that you might not have been able to get gain access to before. By using the method, we taught you in his book you can merely send a gift to a potential client and that should immediately open the door for you and your conversation.

Then we covered the four step process from research and planning which obviously we know is important to clearly identify your target market. And I think it's worth pointing it out again that the better you can identify your target market the more likely you're going to be able to connect with them communicate with them and generate more business from them. And no matter what process you choose to profit from your book I've given you multiple different ways that you can deploy certain sales tactics so that you can attract new business.

Whether or not you decide to become a best-selling author the key factor here is that you've actually published a book in your industry. If you choose to attempt to run a best offer campaign on your own there is a chance that you may fail and fall short. If not an exact science there's no exact number of books I can't tell you would have to sell in order to achieve that status but you could still attempt on your own. Ideally we do offer a best-seller service where we can push your book to a best-seller status on Amazon and then Grant you the title of best-selling author. If you're interested in this, you'll be able to reach out and contact me via this link.

Success With Publishing

Katrina, Published Author at 10 Years Old

Katrina at age ten interviewed on CBS Good Morning show because of her book.

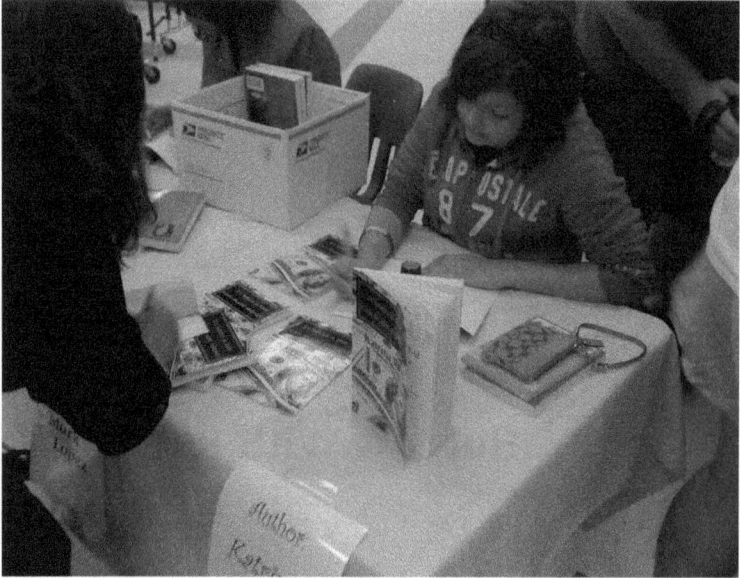

Katrina at age ten autographing copies of her book at a book fair.

Speaking Engagement Leads to Multiple Contracts

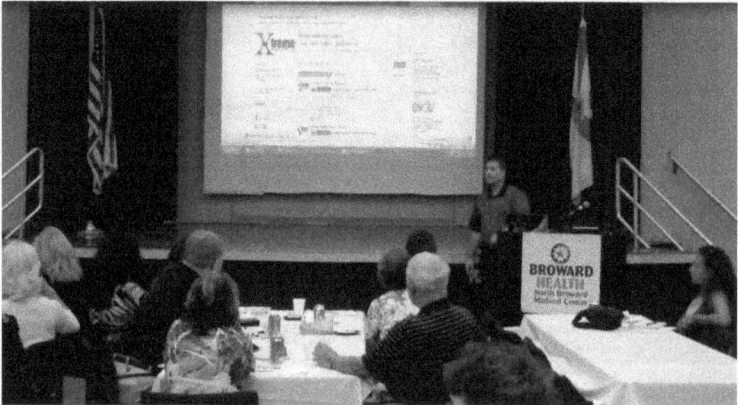

Keith Dougherty Speaking at a Chamber of Commerce Special Event.

Speaking Event Led to $60,000 Contract

Keith Dougherty Speaking at a Business Convention

Codey Become a Best Selling Author Hits #4

Steven and Alexandra Hit #1 Best Seller

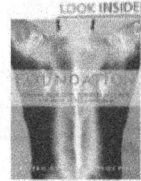

Clients Steven and Alex followed my proven system and becoming #1 best-selling authors.

Jayme Dougherty (Yes, that's my awesome wife.) Hits #1 Best Seller With Her Book

Others that have used Keith's system and published their own books.

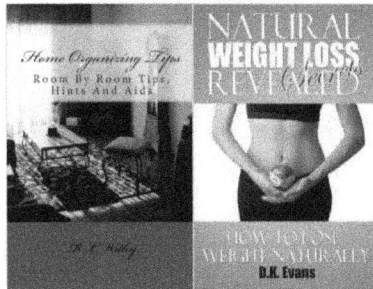

About The Author

"Believe you can and you're halfway there." –Theodore Roosevelt

Keith has over 24 years progressive experience in sales and marketing. As a lead generation expert, Keith strives to implement the most cost-effective automated sales systems to bring new business in a streamlined manner to sustain continue business growth.

He effectively develops and implements targeted action plans to maximize productivity, efficiency and profitability.

His exceptional ability to research and evaluate industry trends and competitor products and use findings in designing and executing innovative strategies to boost company leveraging.

To reach Keith you can contact him via email keith.dougherty@gmail.com.

www.ingramcontent.com/pod-product-compliance
Lightning Source LLC
Chambersburg PA
CBHW021915190326
41519CB00008B/785